GROUND BREAKERS
BLACK MOVIE MAKERS

AVA DUVERNAY

by Joyce Markovics
and Alrick A. Brown

 CHERRY LAKE PRESS

cherrylakepublishing.com

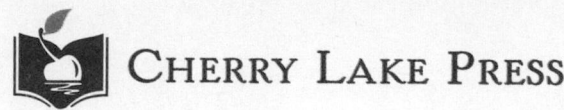
CHERRY LAKE PRESS

Published in the United States of America by Cherry Lake Publishing Group
Ann Arbor, Michigan
www.cherrylakepublishing.com

Reading Adviser: Beth Walker Gambro, MS, Ed., Reading Consultant, Yorkville, IL
Content Adviser: Alrick A. Brown, Film Professor and Filmmaker
Book Designer: Ed Morgan

Photo Credits: © DFree/Shutterstock, cover and title page; © DFree/Shutterstock, 5; © PA Images/Alamy Stock Photo, 6; © Matt Gush/Shutterstock, 7; Wikimedia Commons, 8 © Heidi Besen/Shutterstock, 9; Wikimedia Commons, 10; Mariemaye/ Wikimedia Commons, 11 top; freepik.com, 11 bottom; © hurricanehank/Shutterstock, 12; © CELADOR FILMS/Album/ Newscom, 13; © FS2/Mandatory Credit: FayesVision/WENN/Newscom, 14; Travis Wise/Wikimedia Commons, 15; © CELADOR FILMS/Album/Newscom, 16; © taniavolobueva/Shutterstock, 17; © Stephen Smith/Sipa USA/Newscom, 18; © DFree/ Shutterstock, 19 top; Wikimedia Commons, 19 bottom; © Cubankite/Shutterstock, 21.

Library of Congress Cataloging-in-Publication Data

Names: Markovics, Joyce L. author. | Brown, Alrick, author.
Title: Ava DuVernay / by Joyce Markovics and Alrick A. Brown.
Description: Ann Arbor : Cherry Lake Publishing, 2023. | Series:
  Groundbreakers: black moviemakers | Includes bibliographical references
  and index. | Audience: Grades 4-6
Identifiers: LCCN 2022039528 (print) | LCCN 2022039529 (ebook) | ISBN
  9781668919767 (hardcover) | ISBN 9781668920787 (paperback) | ISBN
  9781668923443 (adobe pdf) | ISBN 9781668922118 (ebook) | ISBN
  9781668924778 (kindle edition)
Subjects: LCSH: DuVernay, Ava—Juvenile literature. | Motion picture
  producers and directors—United States—Biography—Juvenile literature.
  | African American motion picture producers and
  directors—Biography—Juvenile literature. | Women motion picture
  producers and directors—United States—Biography—Juvenile literature.
Classification: LCC PN1998.3.D9255 M37 2023 (print) | LCC PN1998.3.D9255
  (ebook) | DDC 791.4302/33092 [B]—dc23/eng/20221103
LC record available at https://lccn.loc.gov/2022039528
LC ebook record available at https://lccn.loc.gov/2022039529

CONTENTS

THIS IS AVA

"IF YOUR DREAM IS ONLY ABOUT YOU, IT'S TOO SMALL."
—AVA DUVERNAY

Filmmaker Ava DuVernay is an unstoppable force. She makes movies about the experiences of Black people and issues that affect Black communities. An **activist** with a camera, Ava believes in "fighting for **justice**, fighting for good." Since 2008, she has risen to become one of the top Black women moviemakers today. Ava is a leader and inspiration to other filmmakers of color. And this groundbreaker is still going strong.

Ava DuVernay is best known for her work about Black Americans.

Ava became the first African American woman to win the best director award at the Sundance Film Festival. Sundance is one of the most respected film festivals in the world.

EARLY LIFE

On August 24, 1972, Ava DuVernay was born in Long Beach, California. She was raised by her mother, Darlene, and her stepfather. Ava had four siblings. "We lived in Compton, and my mother sometimes didn't want us to go outside," Ava said. "So we would stay inside and create whole worlds." Young Ava loved using her imagination.

Ava and her mom, Darlene Maye

Ava was close to her Aunt Denise who taught her about art. "That was a huge influence on me," said Ava. She and her aunt watched movies together, including *West Side Story* (1961). Ava learned the power of film. And Ava's mom taught her that art could have an impact. "Say something through the arts," her mother would say.

Compton, California, in the 1970s where Ava grew up

Compton is a city in southern Los Angeles. When Ava was growing up, there was a lot of crime and violence. But there was also a lot of beauty. Ava saw both sides of the city.

Ava's birth father, Joseph, was from Alabama. She would spend summers there, not far from the city of Selma. In 1965, before Ava was born, Ava's father saw activists marching from Selma to Montgomery, Alabama. They were led by Dr. Martin Luther King Jr. The people peacefully marched against injustice. At the time, Black people did not have equal rights in America, especially in the South. They faced harsh rules called **Jim Crow laws**. Ava's father talked to his daughter about injustice and the **civil rights** movement. These conversations would later inspire Ava's films.

Dr. Martin Luther King Jr. was a powerful civil rights leader from Alabama. He fought for equal rights for Black people—and all Americans.

The civil rights activists marched over this bridge in Selma, Alabama, in 1965. Police attacked the unarmed marchers.

MAKING MOVIES

In 1990, Ava graduated from high school. When it was time for college, she went to the University of California, Los Angeles (UCLA). There, she studied English and African American studies.

Soon after, Ava got a job at CBS News and as a publicist. In 1999, she started her own company, The DuVernay Agency. Ava worked for movies and TV shows. This is when Ava first became interested in directing films.

The University of California at Los Angeles (UCLA)

During her Christmas holiday in 2005, Ava used $6,000 in savings to make a short film called *Saturday Night Life*. Only 12 minutes long, the film was based on her mother's experiences. It followed a single mom and her three kids shopping at a discount store. The film got the attention of critics.

Ava as a young filmmaker

Ava did not pick up a film camera until she was 32 years old!

Ava then turned to making **documentary** films. In 2007, she directed *Compton in C Minor* about her hometown of Compton, California. According to Ava, the concept for the film was "to capture Compton in only two hours and present whatever she found." The next year, she made a documentary about hip-hop in Los Angeles. It was called *This Is the Life*. Many considered it a must-see movie.

This Is the Life follows a group of hip-hop artists and friends.

"I LOVE THE STORIES THAT I'M TELLING."
—AVA DUVERNAY

Ava behind the camera on a film set

In 2010, Ava wrote and directed a drama called *I Will Follow*. The movie was about her aunt after she got cancer. "I was a caregiver for my aunt, Denise Sexton, in the last year and a half of her life," said Ava. Film critic Roger Ebert called it "one of the best films I've seen about coming to terms with the death of a loved one."

In 2011, Ava wrote and directed another movie that was close to her heart. *Middle of Nowhere* follows a Black woman who drops out of school to support her incarcerated (in-KAHR-suh-reyt-tid) husband. Ava shows both the husband and wife as victims of an unfair system. Or, as Ava put it, "the life that families live as invisible prisoners."

Ava stands in front of *Middle of Nowhere* poster at the movie's premiere.

"THE LIVES OF BLACK PEOPLE, OUR VERY BREATH, OUR VERY **DIGNITY**, OUR VERY **HUMANITY**, ARE VALUABLE AND MATTER TO THE WORLD."
—AVA DUVERNAY

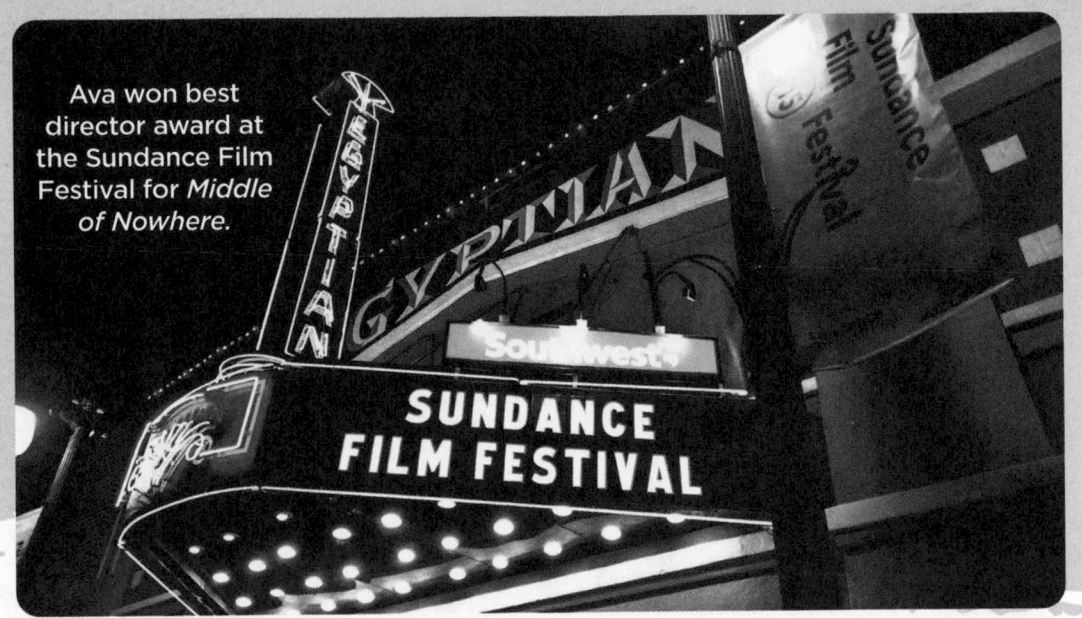

Ava won best director award at the Sundance Film Festival for *Middle of Nowhere*.

"The idea of looking at the victims of incarceration—the mothers, sisters, and daughters—really came out of knowing women who were going through it," said Ava. Film professor Michael T. Martin called Ava's work, "a call to action." He also described her as the "**vanguard** of a new **generation** of Black filmmakers."

To be incarcerated means to be held in a prison. The United States incarcerates more people than any other nation in the world. This is called mass incarceration. Not everyone is treated equally in this country. As a result, there are many more people of color in prison.

Ava working on the set of *Selma*

Inspired by Ava's summers in Selma, Louisiana, she went on to direct a movie called *Selma*. The film covers the 1965 civil rights marches her father **witnessed**. It features Dr. Martin Luther King Jr. and other civil rights leaders. *Selma* was released in 2015 before the 50th anniversary of the marches. The movie was a big hit. It was **nominated** for many awards, including two Oscars and four Golden Globes.

"THE GOAL IS TO SHOW THE DIFFERENT DIMENSIONS OF US."

—AVA DUVERNAY

After *Selma*, Ava was invited to direct Marvel's *Black Panther*. But she said no. "We had different ideas about what the story would be," Ava later said. Ava then made a documentary called *13th*. Some critics would call it her most important movie.

A press conference for *Selma*

Colman Domingo
(Schauspieler/Actor)

Ava DuVernay
(Regisseurin/Director)

David Oyelowo
(Schauspieler/Actor)

Selma was the first major movie about Dr. Martin Luther King Jr.

The film *13th* is about racism, justice, and mass incarceration. The title is based on the U.S. Constitution's Thirteenth Amendment, which outlawed slavery. The movie forces viewers to look at American history with clear eyes. It lays out how the unfair treatment of Black Americans led to the incarceration of more than 2 million people. Ava urges the people watching *13th* to take action to change the system.

Ava and the musician Common at the opening of *13th*

"THE WHOLE FILM IS A **VIRTUAL** TOUR THROUGH RACISM."
—AVA DUVERNAY

In 2018, Ava directed a very different kind of movie. The film is based on the young adult novel, *A Wrinkle in Time*. It follows Meg Murray, a young girl who travels through space and time to save her father.

Ava picked Storm Reid, a young Black actress, to star in *A Wrinkle in Time*.

Madeleine L'Engle wrote *A Wrinkle in Time* in 1962.

AVA'S IMPACT

> "DON'T BELIEVE EVERYTHING YOU THINK. . . . CHALLENGE AND EXPAND YOUR VIEW OF THE WORLD AND YOUR EXPERIENCES."
> —AVA DUVERNAY

Ava DuVernay continues to create films that make a difference. "I'm honored to be making art during this time," said Ava. And she's proud to see other Black people making great art too. Artists of color are expressing themselves and telling their *own* stories. Ava believes everyone must play a part in changing the world for the better. "I want people to be having their own conversation about it," she said. "That's my great hope."

Ava is a huge inspiration to many Black women and girls. She founded ARRAY to support young filmmakers of color.

In addition to being a filmmaker, Ava also creates and directs TV shows. One is called *Queen Sugar*. Ava hired 35 women directors to work on the show, including groundbreaking filmmaker Julie Dash.

FILMOGRAPHY

AVA'S FEATURE MOVIES

2008	*This Is the Life*
2010	*I Will Follow*
2012	*Middle of Nowhere*
2014	*Selma*
2016	*13th*
2018	*A Wrinkle in Time*

GLOSSARY

activist (AK-tuh-vist) a person who fights for a cause

amendment (uh-MEND-muhnt) a new rule added to the U.S. Constitution

cancer (KAN-sur) a serious, often deadly, disease that destroys parts of the body

civil rights (SIV-uhl RITES) the rights everyone should have to freedom and equal treatment under the law, regardless of who they are

critics (KRIT-iks) people who judge or criticize something

dignity (DIG-nuh-tee) a sense of honor and self-respect

dimensions (dih-MEN-shuhns) aspects or features of someone or something

documentary (dok-yuh-MEN-tuh-ree) a movie that recreates actual events or true-life stories

generation (jen-uh-RAY-shuhn) a group of people born around the same time

humanity (hyoo-MAN-uh-tee) kindness and sympathy

Jim Crow laws (GYM KROW LAWZ) unjust laws in the Southern United States that kept Black people separate and prevented them from voting and living in certain places, for example

justice (JUHSS-tiss) fairness

nominated (NOM-uh-neyt-uhd) formally selected to win an award

publicist (PUHB-luh-sist) a person who makes something widely known

racism (REY-siz-uhm) a system of beliefs and policies based on the idea that one race is better than another

vanguard (VAN-gahrd) the leader of a movement

virtual (VUR-choo-ul) for all practical purposes

witnessed (WIT-nissd) saw something

FIND OUT MORE

BOOKS

Blofield, Robert. *How to Make a Movie in 10 Easy Lessons*. Mission Viejo, CA: Walter Foster Publishing, 2015.

Frost, Shelley. *Kids Guide to Movie Making*. New York, NY: Amazon KDP, 2020.

Willoughby, Nick. *Digital Filmmaking for Kids*. Hoboken, NJ: John Wiley & Sons, 2015.

WEBSITES

ARRAY
https://arraynow.com

Britannica Kids: Ava DuVernay
https://kids.britannica.com/students/article/Ava-DuVernay/630857

UCLA Lab School: Ava DuVernay
https://www.labschool.ucla.edu/teach/black-history-american-history/ava-duvernay/

INDEX

ABOUT THE AUTHORS

Joyce Markovics has written hundreds of books for kids. Movies have helped shaped her outlook on life and inspired her to tell stories. She's grateful to all people who have beaten the odds to make great art. Joyce would like to dedicate this book to Sarah Rockett.

Alrick A. Brown is a storyteller and an Assistant Professor at NYU who uses filmmaking to touch the hearts and challenge the minds of his audiences. His creativity is shaped by his time living and working in West Africa, his upbringing in New Jersey, and his travels around the world.